I Pray This Letter Reaches You In Time

Thomas Townsley

Doubly Mad Books

I Pray This Letter Reaches You In Time © Thomas Townsley, 2022

Library of Congress Control Number: 2022947355
ISBN: 978-1-7339321-2-7

All rights reserved. Printed in the United States of America.

No part of this book may be used or reproduced in any manner whatsoever without written permission from the author or copyright holder, except in the case of brief quotations embodied in critical articles or reviews.

First Edition
First Printing

Doubly Mad Books
Utica, New York

Doubly Mad Books is affiliated with *Doubly Mad: Utica's Independent Journal of Arts and Ideas,* both operated by The Other Side of Utica, Inc., a 501(c)(3) organization located at 2011 Genesee St., Utica, NY, 13501.

For more information, write to us at the address above, or go to:
theothersideutica.org
doublymad.org

table of contents

The Allegorist	1
About My Last Poem	2
"How Is Your Tuesday?"	5
Malediction Forbidding Major Thirds	6
Alma Mater	8
By Any Other Name	10
Kaleidescape	12
Yes-Man	14
The Problem With Me No. 74	15
Frigidaire	16
Mauve	18
12 x 12: The Signal Fades	19
The Problem With Me No. 152	29
Bildungsroman	30
Frank's Bad Day (A Pastoral)	31
The Coupon	32
Illusion	34
In Those Days	35
Poem in Which I Spill a Vial of Urania's Tears	36
Summer on Neptune	39
Nocturnal Vignette	47
Exact Change Lane	48
Peace on Earth, Good Will to Men	49
In the Meantime	51
The Jar	54
Suburban Rhubarb	55
Non Oblitus Pater Fuit?	56
The Lie	58
The Problem With Me No. 117	62
Mr. Isn't	64
Plein Air (Last Poem)	66
Big Doin's With All the Fixin's	67

Poem in Need of End Notes	68
Ontological Overbite	70
The Diagnosis	71
The Interrogation	74
The Ordinary	76

Acknowledgements
About the Poet

I Pray This Letter Reaches You In Time

The Allegorist

Begin with landscapes: a river in search of its pocket-watch. Ptarmigan *ex nihilo*. Butterflies shrugging on the amaranthuses.

Irradiant glissandos. Ballerina whispers.

The lantern-girl reminds us: "Origami class is imminent—the body cannot keep its voice." And then, with a wink: "This rhombus was erected to a lesser deity."

The fungus collector agrees. "Most of the stars in this hemisphere are of the Phillips-head variety," he confesses, keeping one hand carefully hidden.

Wild zippers rustle in the barberry hedges.

Things are and are not. Circumstances prevail.

Zithers of light bombard the compound, summoning urgent sforzandos from the shy coxswain.

The new chef reminds us that many dreams lack a narrative thread. He wants you to try his new sauce—now!

And, as always, the Allegorist sits, legs dangling, at the dock's edge, staring at something in the water.

About My Last Poem...

1.

I wasn't myself when I wrote it.

But then, how could I be?

As it turns out, the panopticon was closed.

Shadows fell early and often, refusing points of contact with the objects that cast them.

The moon said, "Not this time, Jack."

Midway through the first draft, my mind drifted off to the Vale of Kashmir, where humidity is on the rise.

Ah, the snow-capped Himalayas!

Sometimes the vehicles for thought become obstacles to it.

Sometimes the lesson pain teaches us is more pain.

I heard a voice whisper, "Maybe you're holding the book upside down."

Did you expect to be loved "for yourself"?

Who strung this black crepe over the public domain?

It's time we acknowledge the Death of the Reader.

It's time we dismantle the central tower.

"Don't you know that the algorithm is continually rewriting itself?" said the one-eyed ogre in the basement. "We no longer need a central tower."

2.

The poem wasn't itself when I wrote it.

Does anyone know enough to be an author?

Each of us carries a piece of Babel in our hands.

I tried to separate the sufferer from the witness, the dream from the dreamer, but they were hopelessly entangled like the two sides of a metaphor which, together, point to an unspoken third term.

"Please don't ask me to wink," said the moon. "It's embarrassing."

Have you heard about the man who "revised" Rorschach ink blots in order to "erase ambiguity" and make clear to anyone "with eyes to see" that they were butterflies?

I drift toward Zero Bridge. Beneath the waters of the Jhelum can be heard a constant murmuring, as of words waiting to be spoken.

3.

You weren't yourself when you read it.

You thought you were reading a Rorschach ink blot.

"One anticipates symmetry, at the very least," you said. "But it seems you have forgotten to fold the page in half. I'm not even sure it's fractal. How is one to interpret it?"

One isn't.

Did I mention that the panopticon was closed?

Did I mention that I proceed by echolocation?

"To know the answer in advance is to fail to live the question," said the one-eyed ogre, gluing together pieces of the mirror my poem broke.

It's time we acknowledge the Death of the Text.

Seen from our drifting houseboat, the Himalayan range forms a striking visual panorama, reflected in the Jhelum's calm pools, but they are treacherous and life-threatening when experienced directly from their peaks.

"You don't say," sneered the moon.

I can admit it now: my last poem never reached Zero Bridge.

My last poem reveled in its failures, which it posited as your failures.

Dare we reread it?

Even now, inside the chrysalis of my last poem, the algorithm, which I did not author, begins to writhe. It is finished tallying our desires and fears—and wants more. As it searches among the shadows for the Right Word, fissures appear along the length of its chitinous shell. Soon its diaphanous wings will emerge from their casing. Soon it will be free to give us the gods we deserve.

"How is Your Tuesday?"

A uniformed elevator operator from the 1940's sits on a footstool, muttering the word "Vatic."

A false prophet leaves something sticky in my inner ear.

A woman who can be seen only peripherally says, "Last night's moon was a decaying tooth, which explains why lies are your foundation. Why don't you—" but her voice is cut short by plummeting chandeliers.

On a deserted beach, I seek another invisible hinge for my collection.

A unicyclist reminds me to examine my choices carefully.

When the salt vendor asks if I believe in love at first sight, I toss seven astrolabes into the sea—then forget what I was going to say.

Malediction Forbidding Major Thirds

Just because I have anatidaephobia doesn't mean ducks aren't staring at me.

They know seven tenths of me lies underwater.

These submerged bells make a sound like the recitative between heartbeats; like the pain between your eyes, transmuted into a valley of black orchids; like a kettle of boiling fissures; like a wasp in a confession booth; like frost forming on your kisses.

I worked for years as a stoker on a steam train—to what avail?

Must imagination remain shackled to memory?

I am Phrygius the Threadbare. Behold my ancestral trombone!

Its gaunt glissando penetrates seven dreams at once.

Your egg basket of microtones and your diphthongs in doll's clothing cannot compare!

Watch me spread moonlight on this saltine cracker as my words approach their boiling point.

I have seen the flagellators descend on wires from their secret fly-tower, disguised as melancholy lovers whose bones glisten with venom.

I have seen Eros wearing a cloak.

I believe if all our synapses fired simultaneously that God's amnesia would be lifted like a cloud.

I am Phrygius the Threadbare. I believe we are all under surveillance.

This morning I found a wood duck feather in my Ovaltine, and an ill wind rose from the sinkhole in my flowerbed.

O noon siren—would you return to me the things of this world?

Not a single gnat in the cathedral of my brain can comprehend its own extinction.

Now come the muttering anomalies, rubbing mint on their gums, and dragging one foot behind the other as they walk.

Now come the suppurating deacons waving matadors' capes at ontological queries.

Someone has lifted the silver from my hand mirror.

Someone is speaking in your voice.

What of the remembered kiss, the silken tent in the desert, the coral reef of love poems, the spine-fish, the soft palette turned to feldspar?

I am Phrygius the Threadbare. Seven tenths of me remains underwater.

My moods are controlled by a silver cloud I am not permitted to look at.

Can't you see I have spent another poem waiting for you?

My trombone sleeps beneath your bedsheets, a festoon of roses in its fuselage.

Alma Mater

A sinkhole opened up beneath the aspic factory.

"Dacron Only" Zones were established.

A team of psychologists showed up in a blue Toyota and distributed word association tests to the poor. Find a term that links each of the following sets of words:

     1. toadstool   nape   remorse
     2. latent   molasses   succubus

Results were sealed in jars and sent to the capitol for analysis, though a change in administration has delayed the results.

The Town Council voted to keep history nostalgic.

We installed partitions, ate meat soaked in vinegar, and practiced our pushups. We declared the Perseid meteor shower heretical.

Each night, when God's pupils were fully dilated, we dreamt of water—familiar creeks swollen, rivers overrunning their banks, turbulent lakes and tumescent seas—and in these dreams the dead appeared, soaked and forlorn, bearing written messages we could not understand because the ink was running.

     3. efficacious   oblong   cleft
     4. ardent   quarry   somnambulist

Last August, there were unconfirmed sightings of a gray angel, hovering silently above the 5 and 10 Cent Store, its open mouth a perfect circle from which no hosannas ushered.

Afterwards came an outbreak of phantom pain and verbal aphasia.

We decreed that single girls of childbearing age must smell of camphor.

We formed a committee to study effulgence.

We added corollary after corollary to a proposition regarding the homeopathy of moonlight as a cure for aspect blindness.

We bore our glandular deficiencies stoically.

When the murmuring spores blew in from the sea and a second sinkhole swallowed the rendering plant, we saved our questions for another day.

By Any Other Name

I met you by a salt lick in a forgotten fjord, resurrecting parakeets, taking bow to saw, making fast and loose with a street lamp's shadow.

Naturally, I wanted to know more about you.

Magenta was your favorite color, and you its favorite person; you lived for that moment when the trumpet player missed a high note so you could shout, "Hey, Sparkles! No noodles for you!"

The Augustan Age was a mere abstraction, at least that's what you said, as another parakeet sprang to life, uttered its small stock of words—"Dasein," "Ereignis," "Ursprung"—and flew into a nearby larch. You strew paste jewelry until my heart felt like Saint Sebastian on a bad day. Then you played "The Summer of '42" on your saw. How could I resist?

Soon, every time you laughed I tasted Benzedrine, and my pockets swelled with periwinkles. My mots justes turned inside out. The northern lights enfolded us but proved meaningless in the ontological sense, like a latticework of clabber, as my heart grew pectoral fins, the better to swim upstream to your roundabout, my dear.

Was this the feeling for which poets suffered cramps? Somehow, my vowels weren't right.

"Hey, Sparkles! Practice your scales!" This yellow parakeet knows only one word: "Zarathustra."

How is it that your touch propels me into a world of plaid?

What's the street lamp got that I ain't got?

Here, have a creamsicle. Sometimes, thinking of you, I pretend that I am a jellyfish—translucent carnivore, like water dreaming itself, just a mouth and venomous tentacles dangling down. "Is it towards you that I move?" etcetera. Don't ask me why I do this—I flunked Chemistry.

Still, I swear by Spinoza's toothbrush, consciousness is not what you or anyone thinks. Sometimes the wrong words work better, but you already knew that, didn't you, Sugar Lump?

Tell that to Alexander Pope, whether he existed or not. Give him a creamsicle, too. I think he would have liked them—in moderation, of course.

Kaleidescape

What a lovely bouffant, I thought, as the Gila monster went on chewing.

Something was askew.

For an entire week I tried to remove the thumbtacks from your spine, while outside, the rain hummed a Dorian scale, drenching my pet ibis. I'd never seen it so forlorn.

"Is that a solecistic rose?" asked a man named Anaphases, who sometimes appeared, clad in a gray raincoat, outside the bay window. He was pointing at something.

Then the call came in from headquarters: "Pick up those chevrons at once!"

A circus-like atmosphere, murky and precipitous, descended on little bat wings upon the cul-de-sac, leaving us to eke out a repressed urge or two in what remained of our quietude.

Who installed these dormer mirrors?

Shall we call this idea "thought-adjacent"?

A scent of overripe guava fruit arose from the aphorism beds, leaving some of us free to weep copiously.

"Of course it's a love poem," she said. "He writes this way to discourage poachers."

"I had these 'dark undercurrents' installed beneath the hummingbirds for maximum exposure," he admitted, before turning his gaze to the rabbit ear antenna. "Perhaps I should tell a tale of my vulnerable adolescence? In the summer of '74, I had a job painting punctuation marks on moth wings—night shifts, mostly, as you might expect. After a while, everything tasted like cardamom. I lived in a dream placenta.

I loitered on boundaries, secreting some kind of tawny mist. Burdock insinuated itself into my plaintive song, alas and alack, and I beheld The Beloved, as if from a crow's nest, amidst tempests of piquant endorphins. No one bothered to explain syllabics to me; no one warned me of the Phoenicians. And that is why you see before you a querulous amateur historian, dabbling in object-relations theories, and waiting for the curdling to subside. Do you understand now?"

Just then, a missive arrived from headquarters: "You're seven chevrons short. Please assume the position."

In my disequilibrium, I found myself pruning the lilacs, waiting for this trochaic longing to overflow its banks, and knowing full well the beautiful maiden always chooses Death as her dance partner—at least here in the valley of the Saxons.

I looked through another window.

Behind the rotating gazebo crouched a chortling poacher. When he caught me looking, he placed a finger on the side of his nose, and intoned, "What are the ideas that never leave you? What are their 'emotional associations,' woof woof? With what familiar tropes do you adorn the wallpaper? With what silver ladle is your 'sincerity' measured? Into what bowl is it poured, woof woof woof?"

Something is askew.

The hummingbirds are coughing. The burdock is blooming. My ibis is nowhere to be found. Death flies overhead in a rented crop duster's plane, trailing clouds of silver confetti and a sky-script message reading "Happy Anniversary, Denise and Karl."

Oh well, we all live by allegories, I thought, as the Gila monster shifted its weight to the hind legs—the better to effect a tearing motion.

Yes-Man

A plastic surgeon with a valise full of milkweed tried to warn me: "The Yes-Man is coming."

Busy dousing pomegranates with kerosene and setting them on fire, I paid no mind.

A libertine phlebotomist in a purple beret was next: "You don't understand. Today's Yes-Man no longer dresses in Tupperware. You won't recognize him by his Dacron smile. Today's Yes-Man is a master of camouflage. He speaks in paraphrase, and behind his eyes are waterspouts that never touch down."

"Very well," I said. "I shall scan the horizon." But instead, I went on lacing corsets for leeches.

Finally, a gaunt perfusionist with fistfuls of tallow assailed me. "Today's Yes-Man dwells in interstitial space," he said. "His love is a dust cloud—his promises, a flight of wrens. When you aren't looking, he'll spread mayonnaise on your soul. He'll make your lilies stammer."

"But Father, my lilies already stammer," I said.

The perfusionist looked puzzled. "I'm not a priest, and I'm certainly not your father," he replied. "I'm here to warn you about the Yes-Man."

"Oh right," I said, and turned back to my private, orthotic lathe.

The Problem With Me No. 74

Time changed the lock on my youth.

Under the zeppelin's shadow, I contemplated the irreducibility of one heart's longing.

I once believed that the living had an advantage over the dead, in that the dead were unaware of their condition, while the living were aware of theirs. Then I began to imagine there might exist an imponderable but pervasive force to which our living blinded us, the same way death blinds the dead to consciousness.

I became a chimney sweep—I mean, a Ferris wheel operator—I mean, a poet.

I made a sacristy of what I believed to be your eyes.

When given the opportunity, I refused to sign on the dotted line, "for the moment of a text's inscription marks a singularity that carries with it a fissuring, a priori"—or so they said in cosmetology school.

I once held your hand in a sensory deprivation tank.

I can never get enough manna.

My past-times include winking, buffing parabolas, extorting empiricists, and bleeding on faulty syllogisms.

My imagined scenarios outnumber my real ones thirteen to one.

"Hey there, dreamer! What are you dreaming about?" the moon asked one night.

"Nothing," I said.

"Hmm. Same here," said the moon, and then one of us went back to sleep.

Frigidaire

A confluence of saturnine impulses beset me as I took the last bite of your egg roll. What you said was true: I loved to explain things. That my explanations were divorced from reality was beside the point. I sighed and reached deep into the Frigidaire, rummaging for my copy of Gichtel's *Theosophia Practica*. The moon ascended—or rather, gave the appearance of doing so.

My hair needed combing. The decision to part it on the left was made long ago, according to social mores I've since forgotten, though passed down by the ancestors, no doubt.

Did you know that Saturn was tricked into swallowing a stone, thinking he'd devoured the son who would depose him? Of course, he had no refrigerator light. One should never eat in the dark; that's the moral of that story! Too obvious? Well, some explanations are like salt on an icy road, designed to provide traction, while others operate on the assumption that desire is fractal.

I heard something stirring behind the pickle jar. "Is that you, Thomas Aquinas?"

Does anyone else believe in plant magnetism—not that it's any of my business?

I seem to be in present tense now, which fills me with foreboding. I'm sorry I took the egg roll you were saving for supper. It was so deep-fried and delicious.

It's time to watch the night birds crisscrossing the moon. Each time they do, another memory becomes inconsequential. You and the blue car. You and the rain. You and—

Mind if I borrow your comb?

Daughter of Nineveh, surround me with your golden sparkles. Proclaim your love in cuneiform! Take in the world with your lying irises, and account me among its denizens. Keep this Frigidaire humming, my little fugitive, my smoke and mirrors, my a priori cuttlefish, my piquant derivative, my pilot light.

Does this jar of stigmata have an expiration date? Forty years ago? I guess I'll risk it—I'm in the mood for something salty.

Mauve

The night we met, the very sight of you caused my dendrites to throw haymakers, sending my nuclei into calypso-spasms.

Methought "How siphon the razzmatazz from your eyes?"

To this end, I vowed to treat our love life as a lion tamer would: I laminated our telos and hung wreathes in the crawlspaces.

I washed the "delicates" with the transubstantiated.

I hid your categorical imperatives in the escritoire—the better to slurp your munificence guiltlessly.

O, no longer would the phrase "In the offing" escape my trembling lips!

Still, my trepidations multiplied.

Would my lovemaking prove too homiletic?

Would you find my bilateral symmetry "predictable"?

It wasn't long before I realized that one of us barely existed—or maybe it took several lifetimes. How long have I been sitting here? Maybe I should have asked your name before living with you for decades in my mind—but alas! our love, refracted through the prism of time, creates no rainbows but remains its original color.

I'm sorry to say that color is mauve.

12 x 12: The Signal Fades

1.

We're having a picnic. Bring your lug wrench.

If you want to see real darkness, look in the pupil of that clown's left eye.

No, the German Expressionists don't come around much anymore. Or maybe they just blend in now.

These permeable membranes are thinner than I thought.

Is that what they call "a gravedigger's moon"?

Please enjoy some starfruit.

I had a bad case of the dithers before the incantations began, but now I feel aphasic.

Would someone inform the author whether he's a site or an origin, so he can choose the proper necktie?

That's artificial mint, Belinda.

The Duchess will see you now. Try not to let on that your hermeneutics has lost its sheen.

2.

Do some words light sparklers in your brain?

The last quarter moon always rises near midnight.

The Duchess keeps mumbling "denouement" in her sleep. What sad pudding fills the bags beneath her eyes?

The static between stations is playing our song!

The corn is high; the moth is on the wing.

Soon open-mouthed October, with its scent of boiling parsnips, its black choir gowns and leather coin purse, will set a bucketful of nematodes outside our door.

Then will our torsos glow with inner light.

I saw Ernst Ludwig Kirchner nibbling a cruller in the 7-Eleven parking lot. He asked me to remind you to return his cerulean blue.

It is said that a linear narrative, in which temporal sequence is taken to signify material causation, carries a particular ideological and political charge.

They've drained the ice dam where I fished as a boy—reduced a four-acre lake to a swamp. Apparently, no one protested, save a few naturalists who were concerned that a rare species of bog turtle might be adversely affected.

Perhaps I'm just dreaming we're asleep.

3.

"Your anamnesis is showing," said the necrologist.

The moon played its silver castanets as her lips pressed hard against the cellophane.

Is that why light coruscated from the last dream of you that I ever had?

The Duchess floats toward the ceiling, high above the circus clown's reach.

A convolvulus vine climbs the walls of the abandoned turret.

Two eyes seek a new head to look out of. Will it be the golem's or the somnambulist's?

What if the mirror wears a mask?

I placed you along this imaginary axis for a reason, my little circuit breaker, my libidinous meringue. Now stop ascending!

One day I shall declaim our love beneath the long spars, as our eyes fix upon the Dry Tortugas.

Till then, try not to confuse Death with the errand boy.

He took her hand. "The spasms are less frequent now," he said. "Thank you."

4.

What you fail to consider is the power of accretion.

Where did all these morning glories come from, anyway?

The narratologists have formed a barbershop quartet—and guess what? They're singing our song, which consists mostly of tritones, with castanet accompaniment.

Erich Heckel reached his fruition as an artist when he learned to give form to negative space, and that, dear reader, is all ye need to know of my aims and intentions.

But hark! Dost thou hear? Cross-eyed October, with its nocturnal drool and its burlap sack for drowning kittens, is soliloquizing on the porch beneath a dysentery moon.

Is its loneliness our loneliness?

Are we trapped forever in the synecdoche of dreams?

Will this inner light guide us down the spiral stair?

Does this nightingale sound funny to you?

"Fortunately for life on Earth, the membranes of living cells are not purely phospholipids. . . ."

"I'll do the coruscating around here!" shrieks the Duchess.

5.

More starfruit?

This lug wrench is an apt symbol of my affection—and, no, I'm not being "Freudian."

Between this sentence and the next lurks the high seriousness of a Rilke poem and several grains of sand from William Blake's loafer.

"Do these tentacles highlight my gestalt?" asks the Duchess, chewing on a clove.

Our father has the latest key fob, and he's double-jointed, too. What does that portend?

Dr. Samuel Mudd, the man who set John Wilkes Booth's broken leg, was imprisoned on the Dry Tortugas until 1869—and that's how much I love you!

Come nostalgia, with your cloud of neurotoxins and your broken mandolins—see if you can lift me off the ground!

I'm the kind of narrator who knows which wine goes best with mayonnaise.

I've heard the humming crystal at the center of the cosmos, though now the signal fades.

I thirst! I thirst!

Send for the errand boy. Tell him my cleft palette has returned.

6.

Long-shanked October, unspool your barbed wire. Sprinkle your black agates on fallow fields. Let the wind spread your aphasia.

My tongue is an anvil.

In one dream, I ask a stranger what time the moon will rise. He hands me a skeleton key. "Bury this in your garden," he says. "Then you'll always know."

"Or you can look in my eye," the circus clown says, winking.

He's brought an artificial rose for you, Belinda.

All I can offer are these morning glories, still clinging to the vine.

The poem always tilts its ear toward what cannot be heard, prefers echo to the original tone.

Now, out of a black tunnel, the eunuch appears. When he raises his lantern, shadows retreat to the hollows beneath his brow. "The spots on moth wings are said to resemble the eyes of predators," he intones.

I place a finger against my lips. "Shhh. Not now."

He nods and blows out the light.

In what passes for darkness, I can feel the narrators walking past each other, murmuring.

7.

In my dream, I am swimming along the ice dam's silty bottom. Or maybe it's in your dream. That would explain why the water turns viscous, why the frogs croak with a German accent, why the lily pads seek to entangle me in their sub-surface syntax.

I suppose we'll learn the answer when one of us wakes up.

Meanwhile, I'm thankful for this trident—and for the purity of thought required to wield it properly. The Duchess says it's a bestowal from the man collecting bog turtles on the shore—or is it from the harlequin swinging on Spanish moss, then crying out for a haberdasher?

"Which of us is the protagonist?" I ask, but they're already boarding a carriage to grandma's house, with its doilies and hints of free masonry and kleptomaniacal roses.

Somewhere in my heart I know that Emil Nolde is being pursued by a golem for his "Nazi sympathies," and my soul is at peace—despite this waterlogged coxcomb.

See how I rub myself with aloe beneath a convalescent moon?
In the blacksmith's shop, they're singing our song, but the time signature keeps changing.

Hare-lipped October, don't come around here cadging drinks with your worn elbow patches and ill-fitting vacuum cleaner attachments. One of them resembles the trident I'm carrying as I move through these dark waters, with the jellyfish of memory, all nerve-endings and venom, floating beside me.

8.

Does anyone recall the word that brought this golem to life?

The denial of narrative may be another way of participating in it.

The moon is always rounding off desire; it is the "O" in our Octobers, my little anaglyph, my *ding und Schatten*.

I keep you on this axis so I can watch it rising in your eyes.

Is there really any need for a story?

Together we observe one of the narrators twiddling his thumbs, repeating the word "erstwhile," and blinking some sort of message in Morse code to the cloud of pink vapor that once was our beloved Duchess.

"Have a seat by this Victrola," says Max Beckmann. "I will paint your portrait. Here, hold this noose. Permit me to light your cigarette. Tell the errand boy to bring another carp."

When, oh when, will we move from meaning to significance?

Just because this light's reflected doesn't mean it isn't real, Belinda.

Let's join hands and form a hermeneutical circle.

This is the story of a star-crossed lover and his dog, Agitprop.

If you keep reading, you might learn how it ends.

9.

"Call me Scooter," he said, but his real name was Karl Schmidt-Rotluff.

"Where would you like this Alizarin crimson?"

"Put it in the special alcove," I tell him. "Don't mind the eunuch."

I wake to find my kidney stones undergoing a Neo-Gothic revival.

"When you live alone with your memories, sometimes pain is the referee," says no one in particular.

Has anyone seen my algorithms?

When the somnambulist says "I," who is speaking—that's what we want to know!

"Some memories are iridescent, like floating oil," sobs the Duchess, who has grown irksome and would be reduced to a plot device by now—if this text had one and was not a train of deformed tropes and trident-wielding narrators.

The expressionists used distortion to present "inner truths," but what happens when the distinction between "inner" and "outer" collapses, when the membrane separating them is shown to be permeable?

"Morning glories live only for a day," says the errand boy, his face streaked with crimson.

Are my dithers returning?

O antihistamine moon, may you ease the scorpion sting of unrequited amours—though not to the point of numbness.

Keep Our Lady of the Imaginary Axis always before me, wrapped in the cellophane of longing, until October comes.

10.

The mirror is in its first quarter phase.

The necessary alphabets are aligned.

I peer into the chasm of you—of your presence, with absence at its center—and nothing is revealed, save the angle of my gaze.

They've drained the ice dam. The Lady of the Lake has gone away. Still, a bog remains—and in the mind, a plumb-line.

Is that a glass eye, Belinda?

Must the moon send down thistles?

I've rearranged these memories so as to block the exits.

Each item in the picture plane must seem inevitable, as must the spaces between them. The same is true of items in a sequence, where negative space becomes negative time, and the illusion of causality, reinforced by habits of language, begs to be maintained. Of course, causality needn't be maintained—or rather, one can explore different sorts of causality, different kinds of inevitability, different ways of using language.

I take a wooded path along the gorge's rim, peer down at the sun-baked rocks in the creek-bed. "This is the present," I tell myself. "And this. And this. And this."

There is no sign of the Duchess.

11.

October, with its black shoelaces, its broken pendulum, its under-bite, its mail order itching powder, and its expired laundry tickets, sets up an ironing board in the narrator's spleen.

The necrologist's pen makes a scratching sound in the dark.

Ponce de Leon, seeker of youth's fountain, discovered the Dry Tortugas in 1513 as he sailed around the Florida peninsula.

What was I searching for when I discovered you?

Have you completed your exegesis yet? Some say it's a pre-condition for hermeneutics, but I'm not sure.

Please watch your step on the spiral stair.

The golem watches the moon spreading its cutlery. He does not search for a word or phrase to describe how it makes him feel. Yet his very life is driven by a word, inscribed on him by another.

His tongue of clay will not speak.

But of what concern is that to us, Belinda, with our Billboard chart memories and mercurochrome kisses?

All this light must be coruscating from somewhere!

And here comes Agitprop, with a carp in his mouth. Good boy! Sit! Now the portrait painting may begin.

Some would say it's not a moment too soon.

12.

The bog turtles are singing our song.

How many narrators did you invite to this picnic, my little parenthesis? Is their loneliness our loneliness?

Did we just dream the humming crystal?

"Your portrait is finished," announces Max Beckmann, with a dramatic flourish. He is covered in blood. "Would you like to see it?"

"Yes," I say.

He turns the easel around so I can observe the canvas. "It was very difficult, very difficult indeed," he says, "But I think I have captured your essence. Don't you agree?"

I stare at what he has painted. "But it's you," I say. "You've painted a self-portrait."

"I call it Self-Portrait with Carp and Trident," he says, sounding a bit irritated. "What else did you expect me to do, under the circumstances—given that you have no face of your own?"

A cheer rises up from the blacksmith's shop. "No face! No face!"

I can hear the errand boy snickering.

Are you still there, My Lady of the Imaginary Axis?

In his alcove, the eunuch applies the first layer of clown makeup—a task for which he no longer needs a mirror.

A trope-free moon rises in the eastern sky.

The last slice of starfruit is consumed. The morning glories blink out, one by one.

Bald-pated October, with its diary of crossed-out words and its suitcase of ventriloquist dummies with real baby teeth, bursts through the front door, licks its lips and begins to hunker down.

The Problem With Me No. 152

As I ascend the stairs, I always pass myself coming down.

I know very few sea yarns.

I forgot to order that box of votive candles you wanted.

What I thought was love turned out to be a sort of emotional flinching—reflected in my syntax and in the nickname you gave me, "Mr. Staccato."

"Mr. Staccato—why so many umlauts?"

"Mr. Staccato, don't put starch in that!"

"Mr. Staccato, what have you done with my paper punch?"

I've been told that my self-fascination is "compensatory"; perhaps that is why I collect other peoples' pre-existing conditions and keep them in glass display cases.

I believe that butterscotch lozenges are the most emotionally distant candy, followed by nougat.

When I say the word "I," a cloud of squid-ink erupts from my mouth. Have you noticed?

Lately I've observed that all my dreams have electric fences—whether to keep me from getting in or getting out remains unclear.

Bildungsroman

Due to the lotus shortage, I got a job painting carousel horses.

The pay was steady, but by the end of summer I'd begun adding blood to their mouths and white crescent moons of fear to their eyes.

A travelling exhibition of Rimbaud's crab lice persuaded me to set my sights higher.

"The complete derangement of the senses!" I shouted. "That's the ticket!"

I joined an Edmund Spenser study group. Each week we smoked another canto of *The Faerie Queen*. It didn't take long to begin seeing things allegorically: the weather, my wristwatch, my father's lance collection.

Then a bad case of synesthesia caused me to smell corn muffins every time a Virtue was extolled.

A life of profligacy followed.

My new lover kept a shelf of memento mori above her bed, illumined by a black-light.

Once you've made love during a Gesualdo madrigal, there's no going back.

So I didn't.

Instead, I underwent centaur surgery. It was unsuccessful.

I received an invitation to a Japanese Tea Ceremony. "Am I Zen enough?" I wondered. On my way there, I discovered a seashell in my pocket and could not recall where I found it.

"Probably Jersey," said a passing yo-yo vendor who'd been reading my mind all along.

Frank's Bad Day (A Pastoral)

He emerged from the arboretum, bloodied, clutching a wicker basket overflowing with Dutchman's pipes.

He squinted against the light. Red toothpicks fell from a misshapen cloud. "What does this sparrow's zig-zag flight portend?" he wondered.

Later that morning, the confession booth he occupied was transformed before his eyes into a sensory deprivation tank.

In the ensuing darkness, tiny, licentious bells began to ring, and he walked the plank of every thought. Soon his signet ring was secreting purple musk.

"Time to practice your scales," the ancestors whispered.

At the Dowager's Picnic, he found himself craving granola. The air bristled with the sounds of pennywhistles and crinkling candy-wrappers. One of his imaginary lovers turned to him and said, "Even the light that surrounds you grows fatigued—and there's always a tunnel at the end of it."

"That hurts my feelings," he cried. Then he fled to a nearby glade, where he watched the leech gatherers circle a bleeding metronome.

The Coupon

October. The trees are screaming.

I receive a letter. Inside the letter is a flyer that promises to "decipher the unknown."

It contains a single coupon, redeemable at the local pharmacy.

When I get there, the line stretches out the pharmacy's door and around the parking lot. Everyone has a coupon. I take my place.

A woman wearing an eye-patch whispers in my ear: "How long will the mind and body go on blaming each other?"

Her voice is a splash of ice water. I'm wiping it from my face when a passing dirigible showers us with confetti. People stand with their palms facing upwards. A man carrying a unicycle bumps against my shoulder. He turns and glares. "My secret alphabet has more letters than yours," he announces.

"Oh yeah? Behold my omphalos!" I snarl, raising my shirt.

It rains for several days. The sewer grates are humming.

Everyone's turning translucent, and the line doesn't appear to be moving; if anything, it's grown longer.

Soon the air is filled with the scent of empty church pews.

Power lines bow under the weight of a descending pall.

Something scurries across the back of my throat.

Darkness rises to meet us.

Another night: unscrambling moonlight, hanging a dead man's ornaments in the bell tower.

Did you know there's a special orchid that must be watered with human tears—its name perpetually forgotten?

"These glass teeth never go out of fashion," shouts the red-bearded minister, as if daring me to set his bible on fire.

So I do.

Now I can no longer remember why I'm here, but it doesn't matter. The smoke angels are beautiful because they're crying.

Illusion

"It was just the illusion of a mirage—not a real mirage. And besides, I wasn't thirsty," I told the warden. But then I realized that the warden was just an illusion of a warden, not a real one. "Does this mean I'm not in jail?" I wondered—and sure enough, the bars turned out to be illusions, too. "I'm free," I thought. "Finally, my oppression is ended." And for a moment I was filled with great joy. But, of course, you can imagine what happened next, can't you? My freedom turned out to be illusory, too. Ditto for my joy.

And this "you" I'm addressing—what about you? You claim we met in line at the Savings and Loan, that we had similarly colored parakeets, that we both wore thimbles in times of stress, and that our love-making was a form of controlled psychosis—but now I see that you've begun to shimmer around the edges, too.

"Oh yeah?" you say. "What about you? Looked in any mirrors lately?"

"You mean have I looked in the *illusion* of a mirror," I say, and we both laugh, clicking our thimbles together and listening intently as our parakeets recite these words.

In Those Days

It seemed that people were always being rescued by collies.

Everything tasted like hydrangeas.

Radios picked up signals from space—from what we called "space," though it really wasn't, as we later learned—and crickets sang "Ave Maria" in the turnip fields.

Our moods were controlled by ions and experimental breakfast cereals.

At night, the creature in the wardrobe closet sometimes woke us with its garbled song. We tried not to listen, but later we found ourselves humming it as we cruised the back streets, looking for innocents.

Poem in Which I Spill a Vial of Urania's Tears

As I look on, the beast wraps its venomous tentacles around the military academy's dormitory.

Then it lets loose a terrible roar and begins to squeeze the concrete walls, cracking them like a mollusk shell to get at the meat inside.

"Why must I be a spectator to this sort of thing?" I wonder.

Wouldn't it be better to imagine a world where we all carry pitch pipes and chew with our mouths closed—a world where monorail rides are free and children speak in iambic pentameter?

In such a world, there's a place for you and me. We could stroll barefoot through a nearby botanical garden—say, the one behind the armory—and then I could ply you with my "rude song" and make my feelings clear, accompanied by this here 21 chord autoharp; it's an Oscar Schmidt—top of the line, in case you were wondering.

"Your feelings seem somewhat mixed," you tell me. "I'm picking up lust, to be sure, but your affection seems suffused with ennui and self-doubt, marked by passive-aggressive behavior. I'm also sensing guilt—lots of super-ego issues."

"This here autoharp can handle it," I reply. "It plays both major and minor chords. Dominant sevenths, too, in case we're feeling exotic." I wink.

Then I notice the trees bristling with glass birds. All around me is the sound of wind chimes.

"Uh oh. This can't be good," I think. "What now?"

Someone hands me a bar of pumice soap.

The sky loses consciousness.

For several minutes, I am alone on an alluvial plain, pondering the word "nascent." I chant it over and over, first in my mind, then under my breath. Soon I am emphasizing the "s" sound, like a hissing snake. "Nassssssscent. Nasssssssscent."

I seem to be wearing some sort of itchy monk's cowl.

"Whose world is this?" I ask myself. "Surely it's not mine."

Gone is my 21 chord autoharp, and gone are my thoughts of you.

Then I hear it: somewhere along the distant horizon, Urania is weeping. Immediately I get down on my hands and knees and begin to crawl toward her—not that I want to, but something compels me. That's how it is with goddesses, especially the ones who are part Titan and part Olympian—they don't give you much choice.

I crawl and crawl. My hands and knees have taken on the color and texture of overripe pomegranates. "Why must she be so distant? She's just like her sisters. They all play hard to get. But maybe there's a good reason for that," I tell myself.

When I reach her, I keep my head bowed and do not presume to stare at her face or starry cape.

She must sense my presence because the weeping stops. I feel the weight of her gaze upon me. It's the equivalent of a large sack of potatoes, or maybe a couple pecks of bulgur.

She sets the vial of tears beside me. "Is this what you seek?" she asks. "I wasn't seeking anything," I say—then, afraid I've offended her, I try to cover my tracks. "I mean, I'm honored, of course. Who wouldn't be? A goddess's tears! Wow!"

"Most of my tears become stars," she says. "The stars were the first abstract signs. But no one remembers that now."

"I guess I never thought of it that way," I reply. And this is when it occurs to me that maybe I was never meant to be a poet. Maybe I was never meant to be a hierophant, a minstrel, a skald.

Simultaneous to this revelation, I find myself where I started, back at the academy watching myself watch these poor cadets writhing on the lawn as the beast's venom does its work. The beast is watching, too.

When it lets go another roar and turns its scaly head to face me, I cover my ears and close my eyes.

The bell hop taps me on the shoulder. "Will you be staying another night, sir?" he asks.

I blink and look around. I seem to be in a hotel lobby, rather opulent, with a black and white checkerboard floor, plush chairs, and a grand piano. The bell hop, decked in a red uniform, looks at me expectantly, hands on hips. His face and neck are covered in oddly shaped welts, like some sort of hieroglyphs. I catch myself staring, as if trying to read them, and quickly avert my gaze. "It's hard to say," I tell him.

But it's too late. I think he saw me looking because his smile goes brittle around the edges. "Everything is hard to say, isn't it, sir?" he replies.

Summer On Neptune

1.

It's summer on Neptune.

Everyone's eating radishes.

The horizon keeps blinking.

Why won't you manifest—not even a little bit?

"Don't let those divining rods get in the wrong hands," says Freder. "You know what happened last time."

Do I?

I could go for a nice glissando right now.

What rhymes with "inchoate"? What rhymes with "unabated storm"?

From where you are, you'll need a small telescope to see us—so we're told.

We have no coal on Neptune, but we have diamonds aplenty—though not the "girl's best friend" variety.

We also have no ontology, no old women selling lint, no Pascalian wagers.

Our marsupials aren't cute.

Our songbirds appear rarely, for which we are grateful, since they are harbingers of death.

We earn our living watching pressure gauges. We send the data back home, where some say it is recorded in a ledger.

We've evolved to have a third eye, but it remains closed.

What I wouldn't give for some snap-peas!

We have no word for "adagio," no word for "disambiguate."

Sometimes our fourteen moons befuddle us; maybe that's why we count no higher than we need to.

Our single epistle from Earth, a love letter hand-written on bleached parchment, is enshrined in the Tourist Center, now under renovation.

"Don't tell them about the feral children," whispers Freder, conspiratorially.

Did I mention that we have no color red— the red wavelength is entirely absorbed by the atmosphere, making it hard to fall in love.

I once saw a photo of a sumac tree from Earth; this experience resulted in mixed feelings and uneasy dreams.

Therefore I am led to believe that sensations exist about which no one has told us.

2.

Captain Starview will be addressing you shortly, with details of your mission. Please stand by.

What rhymes with "demythologize"? What rhymes with "albatross"?

Did you know that Neptune is the only planet in our solar system whose existence was predicted by mathematics prior to its discovery in 1846?

Is it any wonder we've been chosen to monitor the gauges?

Some would argue that physical objects can exist without ideas, but ideas can't exist without physical objects. Others—though admittedly fewer—would argue the opposite.

We would prefer not to argue at all.

Our celery has horizontal fibers.

Our eels are bilingual, albeit telepathically.

Who will comb the horizon's eyelashes beneath these fickle moons?

"Don't tell them about our peripheral vision," Freder warns. "Think of what they might do with such knowledge."

I won't.

Instead, I'll think of the sumac's tumescent seed pod, with its blush of a harlot's lipstick.

Did I mention that our dreams are perpendicular to yours? How this came about is hard to say, except to note that one cannot get here without first undergoing a state of suspended animation, the long term effects of which we are only beginning to understand—like a loss of onomatopoeia or a fervent saltiness.

Or a refusal to manifest.

All of which makes our relationship rather one-sided.

Still, let no one accuse me of a priori thinking! Clearly, this memory of you has left an aftertaste, like lithium.

I'm told our summers last forty years, which should give us time to work things out.

Meanwhile, let's all welcome the word "redolent" to our little colony. Your call is very important to us. We appreciate your patience. Captain Starview will be with you momentarily.

I hope this doesn't take too long. I'd hate to miss the conversion ceremony.

3.

We live amidst shades of blue—a color "always in retreat."
Our emotional palette ranges from cobalt to cyan—azure to cerulean during estrus.

On Neptune, one year lasts two lifetimes—maybe yours and mine put together!

Nothing here is completely opaque—except, as the saying goes, "the differences between us."

Watching our narcissi bloom may lead to bouts of authorial intention—allegorically speaking.

No one understands why the wind hasn't ground us to powder—or the burning cold reduced each heart to a crystal.

"Don't practice your gaze in front of outsiders," warns Freder, pointing to a figure on the horizon—or is it a reflection?

According to my research, the sumac is considered an invasive species on Earth, capable of cloning itself by means of rhizomes, which form an elaborate underground root system—cut it down in one place, and it will spring up in another, like these images of you.

Have I mentioned our six rings, far less satisfying than Saturn's—comprised primarily of space debris and regret?

Do you think it is easy to maintain "living conditions" here at the edge of the solar system—where the distance between ideas and physical objects is both razor thin and infinite?

And having said that, do you think these gauges are accurate—or that these grafts will take?

4.

Please stand by. Captain Starview will soon be spinning the hits, laying down the platters that matter!

I am with you—with the idea of you, my little horizon—here in the blue.

I see you now, with your face like fourteen moons, illumined by a blue candle.

I see you in your many phases, in your distances, in your play of light and shadow in the dark wing of night.

I see a long line of exegetes trailing after you, interpreting each gesture.

What would they make of the glissando of emotions you've caused me to feel? Would they dare affix a single word?

What rhymes with "convulsive"? What rhymes with "coagulate"?

How many years has it been since we touched—and Earth years or Neptunian years?

Does this gravitational pull I'm still feeling connect me to an idea or a physical object?

"Don't ask them," Freder hisses. "How are they supposed to know? Besides, in exile, does it really matter? Now go recalibrate your gauges!"

"Why wouldn't they know?" I think to myself—but naturally, I do as I'm told.

I'm not yet ready to admit my growing suspicions: that no one remembers we're here, and that these gauges we watch perpetually aren't attached to anything.

5.

Our midnight-blue roses make a swallowing sound.

Our dreams leave a residue that accretes the way stalactites do.

We are studying your concept of irony, but we find it difficult to understand.

Is this why we have no word for "metalepsis"?

We have come to realize, however, that the horizon is neither a physical object nor an idea, strictly speaking. It is a necessary illusion, marking a real limit of perception.

We're forming a committee to study the phenomenon.

Could it be that "redness" marks another kind of perceptual horizon—and "you" another still?

"Don't extrapolate too much," warns Freder, looking up from his plate of scallions. "Don't try to make this into a 'closed' text. Don't count your bruises. Don't close the narrative distance. Don't trim the narcissi. Don't touch that dial. Don't look up 'tidal locking'—not with fourteen moons! Don't pull the wool over my third eye. Don't leave any radishes behind, or else you'll attract songbirds. Don't leave the gauges unattended. Don't forget what brought you here—or if you do, then don't forget that you've forgotten."

"These bruises may have occurred during transit," I tell him.

"Don't dwell on them," he says. "They probably occurred while you were in suspended animation."

Of course, I remember nothing of that. What I do know is, once I woke up in this blue world, I still remembered you—and that is how I remembered myself. How far I've carried both of those memories—or how far they have carried me! Freder would probably warn me not to trust them; he'd explain how memories are subject to "tricks."

We gaze up at the fourteen moons, strewn like scattered change across the sky.

"Is it time for the divining rods?" I ask.

"Don't bring them out until the conversion ceremony has begun," Freder says. "By then, the outsiders will be gone. Only true Neptunians are permitted to observe it."

At the mention of "true Neptunians," I can feel my third eyelid begin to twitch.

6.

Please stand by. Captain Starview is waiting in the wings with a message for all you gauge gawkers.

What rhymes with "heliotropism"? What rhymes with "parallel processing"?

The love letter from earth reminds us that "failure to manifest" may be an essential ingredient of "long-term emotional interest" for certain personality types.

Is this why I see you, always in the distance, where mirages dwell, holding a basket of snap-peas?

Some of us have come to understand that each perception is also an act of interpretation.

Others still believe a true glissando is possible.

It is hard to remember the specific events which brought us to this place—this blue condition. Nor have we any way of recalling how long our suspended animation lasted—or how we dreamed our way out of it—since time here is no longer sequential.

But it's summer on Neptune.

This cold should be lethal, yet here we are.

We have no first causes, no bank clerks in clown suits professing anagogy, no word for "sublimate."

Our escarole tastes metallic, and our marsupials remain hideous.

Our fourteen moons will vex your dreams, if you are still capable of having them.

I would offer you more radishes, but the divining rods are picking up a signal.

I believe the conversion ceremony is about to begin, and the rules are clear: only true Neptunians may attend.

Try not to stare directly at the feral children on your way out.

"Yes! And don't tell them about your scotoma," Freder hisses, chewing on a leek. As he talks, little pieces of it spray from his mouth. "Don't tell them that our rings are incomplete or that seeing them is a trick of perceptual closure. Don't tell them our myths are purely aesthetic. Don't offer them a symptomatic reading. Don't let on that desire must always be satisfied by symbolic substitutes for that which it cannot possess. Don't tell them about Captain Starview's club foot. Don't tell them what the Phoenician sailor means."

"Why would I do any of that?" I wonder, as I am lowered onto a gurney.

Someone is palpating my cephalic vein.

Awake, my rhizomes! Man the gauges!

It's summer on Neptune.

The horizon is blinking, and everything is redolent of you.

Nocturnal Vignette

"Excuse me, Mrs. Battendorf," said the moodily aloof interrogator, "but how do you like your ptarmigan? Pan broiled? Over easy?"

Mrs. Battendorf had the look of one who's seen many precipices. "Is it night already?" she asked.

The interrogator drew back the velvet curtains.

Outside, the moon was writing codicils in unleavened light.

From the steeples, the usual angels uttered prepositions through bloodless lips. It was the only Part of Speech they knew.

Meanwhile, in the churchyard, the sexton was digging up the body of his ex-lover, as he did every night around this time, while a jackal-headed god looked on.

Mrs. Battendorf smiled. "I'm going to put on more lipstick now," she said.

When she reached into her purse, the interrogator began to twitch like a dreaming dog.

Exact Change Lane

Midnight was your true north, until they declared your compass unfit to stand trial.

Now I am accused of dreaming you into transparency. Well, *mea culpa*.

The red wizard, seven feet tall, who works as a toll collector, reminds us that the implicit telos of our rhetoric must be resisted. "Have you observed how the margins are constantly shifting?" he says, thrusting out his hand.

He has a face of charred wood and mirrors for eyes.

"Why do I feel like I've been here before?" I ask him.

"Because you have," he says. "Third time today. That'll be seventy-five cents."

"Third time? Why can't I remember? Am I lost?"

"What do you think?" he says.

"I think that if this is the third time, then you already know I can't pay—right?"

He smiles and withdraws his hand. The toll gate rises.

"Of course," he says. "But it's nice to hear you admit it."

Peace on Earth, Good Will to Men

"Whoever hung this tinsel clearly never suffered like the rest of us," Mother said. She plucked a strand and rubbed it between her fingers. "Maybe we could use it to snare birds."

"Feeling sublunary, are we?" Father chirped, squinting through his bifocals at a crossword puzzle. His pen scratched and scratched. "What's a five letter word for 'a distanced and postponed verisimilitude?'"

As he spoke, three silvery shoehorns floated into the room on silken parachutes.

"See that? I told you to call the roofers," Mother said. "Or maybe the exterminator."

"Now, Mother, stop worrying your noggin!" said Father. "Why don't you try on those new earmuffs? Why don't you slip into that black and white dress? Why don't you see how small you can curl up? Why don't you read the *Book of Lamentations*? Why don't you study your reflection in a toaster? Why don't you eat that custard you brought home from the jubilee? Why don't you quell your sudden gusts? Why don't you deep fry something oblique? After all, it's soon feeding time—isn't that right, Junior?"

Mother looked at me. "Why are you here?"

"I'm not!" I shouted. "I'm not anywhere!"

"You'd better not be! I found blood in the pantry this morning. I told you what would happen if you—"

"But the moon!" I cried. "Last night, I lay prostrate in its barbed light. I was beset with blue isotopes that took my astral secretions at neap tide. My hormones buzzed. I heard a distant trombone. I longed to return to the gully, to touch wet fur, to render immobile the turning cogs of ecstasy."

"Stop blaming the moon!" Mother shrieked. "Who taught you to talk like that? I ought to bleach your tongue!"

"There, there, Mother," said Father. "He's a growing boy. Why don't you go polish a fulcrum? Why don't you coddle an oscilloscope? Why don't you take a float trip in your new red dinghy? Why don't you—"

"Shut up! Shut up! Shut up! Why don't you go dig a trench?" screamed Mother, her black lips drawn back and quivering.

Father arched his back and hissed. His dewlap became engorged.

How much longer must I go on narrating this? I wondered.

Another shoehorn floated into the room; it paused and hovered directly in front of me.

"Please stand by for a subliminal hum," it said.

In the Meantime

(And that is why our hero appeared in front of middle management, wrapped from head to toe in aluminum foil, chanting "I'm a people person" and waving a thesaurus from which all the Q-words had been torn and set afire.)

(In the meantime, you combed your beard of ignis fatuus, as gray birds sang "No comment" from the trees.)

("This is an inauspicious start," you thought. "Perhaps we should wait for the narrator to arrive—though not the narrator who extracts gold shavings from his navel/nor the one with whisk brooms for hands/nor the one who builds a terror—I mean tower, with its premeditated view of the parking lot...")

(The whole must be grasped piecemeal, through its constituent parts, as well as through the gaps—temporal and spatial—between them)

(—which is to say the whole cannot be grasped)

(—which is to say she sprinkled talcum powder on my ennui)

(—which is to say "What kind of flower best serves this text?")

("What phase moon?")

("What is your favorite passage from Paul's *Letter to the Ephesians?*")

("Is this a good place to insert a Tristan chord?")

("Not the fat-fingered narrator I saw on mother's black & white TV, spinning dinner plates atop sticks/not the "everybody's uncle" narrator foisting breath mints on children/not the indigenous tribe of narrators from The Island of Polymorphia with their bone necklaces and thirteen kinds of syncopation/not the narrator who burnt his tongue on soup...")

(And so our hero shaved the burgermeisters' eyebrows and kept the hair in a coin purse, which he carried in his waistcoat as he rode a flaming gondola to the enterprise zone's far shore, reading "The Wanderer" aloud and pausing every so often to cry "Tell the committee my mind is all abundance!")

(In the meantime, you made sure the *deus ex machina* wires were securely attached, "just in case." You looked forward to pulling the red lever once the narrator arrived—and who could blame you, really, given the prophecy? You repeated the word "subliminal"—I mean "subterfuge"—over and over until it became a warm marble on your tongue.)

(Would the narrator bring a metalanguage? Would there be a play within a play? Would there be diegesis or mimesis or perhaps a third way—a twisting albeit petal-strewn path between them that confounds the surveyor's monitoring prism?)

(She threw the candelabra in the backseat of her used Datsun and drove to the femme fatale tryouts.)

(Should a dream taste of phosphorus?)

(How shall the Tristan chord be resolved?)

("I suppose the blue tongue should have been a clue," said our hero, whom we join in medias res, chopping onions on a sleeping nymph's back, using an old barber's razor from the Sixties. "You can't trust a blue-tongued dog. I don't care if it has a pedigree.")

(In a murmuring echo chamber, I listen to the deep speaking unto the deep...)

("The first sound a meteor hears is the hiss of its own dissolution," said another voice—was it the narrator, arriving at last in a burgundy smoking jacket, with a fistful of moustache wax and buttons for eyes?/the narrator who came of age in The City of Imaginary Footbridges and never knew his real mother and father, though they often appeared in the form of a cloud, whispering instructions, which he carried out to the letter and then immediately forgot?/the narrator who craved Welsh rarebit?/the narrator who said "The problem with most similes is that invention is restricted to the vehicle"?/the narrator who burned the furniture and fired the moving men?/the narrator who descried "the nature of the children of wrath" while operating heavy machinery?/the narrator who sipped moon broth and cleared his throat?)

(—who said, "What is it you think that I can do here"?)

(—who said, "I've been watching you, combing your memory as if combing a beach, looking for sea glass. You understand that sea glass consists of shards worn smooth, made opaque by the water's love? Do you know the difference between sea glass and true gemstones? Must I explain the diaphanous"?)

(—who said, "Your memories are cheap baubles—what translucency they possess is rapidly fading"?)

(—who said, "Your story was over before I got here. Let me go someplace where I might make a difference. Let's put an end to this now. Pull the red lever""?)

(—who said, "I thought you knew: Everything is in the meantime," and left without saying goodbye?)

The Jar

A jar floats past us, down the river.

"See how it floats?" someone says. "It's beautiful!"

"The jar floats because it is pure form—empty of all but itself, its lid tightly sealed," says another.

"But the purpose of a jar is to contain," says a third. "What good is an empty jar to anyone?"

"Do you see how it bobs along so jauntily? Do you see how it catches the sun? If the jar had contents, it would sink like a stone," replies the first.

"Shut up! Shut up!" I cry. "Can't you see I'm trying to write a poem?"

Suburban Rhubarb

Mother's basting the geoduck.
The Reformation has run its course.

Imaginary nasturtiums line real trenches, or so we believe, hey ho!

These Hessians are known for their elaborate centerpieces that make use of fingernail clippings, live sea urchins, and three kinds of granite.

"'An aggressive and playful luxuriation in the non-representational' is characteristic of 'late capitalism,'" said the fictitious lover to the platitudinous mob.

Who doesn't have an Uncle Ulrich?

Thursday deposits its lawn clippings on my tongue.

This canvas cries out for more Titanium White.

Who is that pall bearer no one recognizes?

Why am I developing an antipathy to certain birds?

Come dusk, the communion wafer truck will prowl the cul de sac, searching for lost souls. I pray this letter reaches you in time.

Non Oblitus Pater Fuit?

I've forgotten my father, and now I'm choking on the moon.

Yes, like a dream washed away in morning light, all memories of my progenitor have vanished.

Was he a crop duster or a bear baiter's assistant? A defrocked priest or a jongleur?

Was he a Ferris wheel operator with a red eye-patch and jumper cable clips for hands, or a barnacle scraper who could summon blue angels in his sleep?

Was he the first recorded shapeshifter from Evanston, Illinois, or a lighthouse keeper with a split personality, one of whom wrote love poems in poulter's measure?

And what of his history?

Did the sensation of a scabbard brushing against his thigh during a high school performance of Othello make him shiver in unanticipated ways?

Did the shrapnel in his war wounds once pick up radio signals from an all-night gospel station?

Did he really answer a question about Stephen Mallarme's poetry by removing his glass eye and spinning it like a top on the teacher's desk?

Did he hide his vestigial tail from lovers—or was that how he attracted them?

Perhaps if I could conjure a single image of him, others would attach themselves to it, piece by piece, until a "bigger picture" emerged—a string of memories, like beads on the wire of causation: his florid face, his goggles (or lack thereof), his enormous hands, his great height or imponderable girth, his cuneiform scars, his prosthetic devices, his riding crop, his incessant coughing.

But the moon keeps throwing chalk dust in my eyes.

It smothers my synapses.

Its acrid powder fills my lungs.

All I can remember is that I've forgotten him—that the sequence of memories comprising him has been erased, leaving a father-shaped hole in me. Therefore I am incomplete. And yet that hole, more than anything, defines me.

"Did it ever occur to you that you are just the phantom pain of your father's life, and not the other way around, as you smugly assume?" says the woman in the green dress.

(Sometimes she appears to me, standing in newly opened doorways to darkened rooms.)

"What do you mean?" I ask her. But I know what she will say:

"Perhaps your father has always existed, and your amnesia is a rhetorical gesture."

"Or perhaps he has never existed, and you yourself are a function of language—your words, a constantly deferred search for a proper name."

And she will say it all without moving her lips, which are the most enticing I've ever seen.

The Lie

1.

What was The Lie?

Who told it?

Did I really think it was wrong?

Did it wash over us, like air through a car window?

Did it fall around us like the Perseid meteor shower?

How many were affected by it?

How many never caught on?

And all the lies within The Lie, like Russian eggs—did we take them into account? Or were we too absorbed in metonymic side-stepping—in what they called "verbal sashaying" back in those halcyon days?

(That was before I learned to cure my stammer by parsing speech into musical phrases.)

(Side effects include involuntary carnival-barking and pleated dreams.)

Does my speaking of The Lie make you uncomfortable?

Would you rather I spoke of The Truth—as if it, too, did not have its palimpsests?

"Who are you talking to?" shouts Uncle Gestalt. He's been sniffing the pages of the latest *Poetry* magazine, and seems irritated. "Take your ideal readers and get out of here!"

He shakes a knobby fist and scowls, apropos of nothing—or maybe it's the sight of us sprawled naked on the patio furniture.

I swirl my gin and tonic. "They're implied readers, if you must know," I say.

"I don't care! I can feel their breath on my neck!"

"No you can't. That's a lie, too," I tell him.

"You and your Lie!" He rises from his chair and hobbles toward us, breathing black smoke. "Don't you know that your so-called "Lie" doesn't even exist—and that, in itself, IS The Lie?"

He begins to swat us with his copy of *Poetry*—an issue devoted to formal, metrical verse written by hemophiliacs. One swing cracks me good across the brow.

"Ouch! That hurts!"

"That's the idea," he says.

2.

Is it possible to lie without language?

And with language, is it possible NOT to?

Step right up! Step right up!

Did you believe the lie of the rose, the lie of starlight reflected in a pond, the lie of white birds upon a quaking bough?

Did you believe the lie of capital?

Did it cool your brow like a lover's kiss?

And now--do you believe that every lie is a bridge and every truth a chasm?

Do you believe William Butler Yeats finally realized that Maude Gonne was a lie he told himself repeatedly—as I have come to realize regarding you?

Are we the lies we choose to accept?

That's a nice hat, by the way. I wish all of my inscribed readers wore hats like yours.

Would you like some golumpki? Aunt Prima Facie made it from scratch.

"You all look so hungry," she says. "Why do your readers look so hungry? What have you been telling them? Eat! Eat!"

"Aunt Prima Facie, did you know that the Russians have no word for 'blue,' yet we consider it a primary color. How do you explain that?"

"Stop your nonsense! Look at them! Poor things! Their ribs are showing! Eat! Eat!"

I believe we are Nothing's way of lying to itself.

3.

Is everything we say or write a mirage?

Is The Truth what's left after all the lies have been told?

From the next room, Uncle Gestalt shouts, "You will never know what it's like to 'bleed out' over a poem!"

I have a mouthful of golumpki and do not answer.

My model readers, however, begin to speak.

"The lie of the lighthouse beam."

"The lie of the stammering prophet."

"The lie of the bell tower, smothered in ivy—and of the bell ringer, waiting for a word."

"The lie of the cypress tree silvered by moonlight."

"The lie of the author."

"The lie of the wine-stain on white silk."

"The lie of a lover beckoning from the terrace."

"The lie of the broken compass and the mystical honeycomb and the lute's broken string."

"Stop it!" shouts Uncle Gestalt from the next room. "What do any of you know? Imagine living with the knowledge that the next wound—even the slightest—could be fatal. A paper cut, even! That's the kind of thing to make of a real poet out of you!"

"Now, dear, leave them alone," says Aunt Prima Facie. "Look at them! Is it any wonder they believe in lies? Can't you see that they're starving?"

The Problem with Me No. 117

"You are mentally color-blind," said the leprechaun.

"What do you mean?" I said. "There's nothing wrong with my vision. I see fine. For example, that jacket you're wearing is green."

"Of course it's green! I'm a leprechaun. Leprechauns wear green. Everyone knows that," the leprechaun said. "Therefore your statement proves nothing. Besides, I'm not talking about your external vision. I'm talking about your mind's eye."

"My what?" I said.

"Your mind's eye," the leprechaun repeated. "I believe it is subject to mirages. Tell me, what do you see right now?"

I looked up. Just then, a pair of acolytes hurried past us on the street, carrying their brass candlesnuffers or "emunctoriums" as the *Glossary of Ecclesiastical Ornaments* calls them. But instead of wearing the traditional white robes, each youth was draped in what appeared to be a translucent shower curtain decorated with blue and green goggle-eyed fish.

"They must be late for services," I said.

"What are you talking about?" the leprechaun snapped.

"Those acolytes, also known as 'accensors,'" I replied, pointing. But when I looked again, all I saw was a middle-aged man in a jester's cap, riding a unicycle with a rhesus monkey perched on his right shoulder. The monkey looked straight ahead, unfazed, as if it had done this many times before. The man, however, appeared to be weeping.

"Now do you see what I'm talking about?" the leprechaun said. "Your inner vision is untrustworthy."

"Maybe—but why?" I asked, turning to face him. Of course, the leprechaun was no longer there. I couldn't even remember how to spell "leprechaun" anymore. Instead, an old woman looked up from her xylophone, which she'd set up along the curb right here on the street where, I now realized, I lived.

"Any requests?" she asked.

I stared at the mallets clutched in her knobby fists. They looked like birds of prey.

"Didn't I used to know you?" I asked. "I mean, like, a long time ago?"

"You tell me," she said, but her expression didn't change; it remained stone-like, yielding no clues—not even after she launched into an expressive rendition of "The Shadow of Your Smile" as gold lockets, each bearing the singed hair of a different lover, began to drop from the trees into the mouths of waiting crocuses below.

Mr. Isn't

We fled the Gnostic Jubilee and took refuge among the smitten.

Some of the elders pursued us, so we hid in a mangrove swamp.

We saw Lilith weeping anthracite tears beneath a desultory moon.

A series of pointless gestures followed.

"Can't we get on with the ribbon cutting ceremony?" I wondered.

You called me "Mr. Isn't," and the name stuck.

Meanwhile, some of the elders had sharpened their teeth with a metal file.

"Between any two thoughts lies a third that never reaches consciousness," you said. Were you talking in your sleep again?

I began in earnest to count your eyelashes. The average person has 90 to 150 on each upper lid. How would you compare?

But before I could finish counting, something distracted me.

A screech owl passed before the mirror.

Blue-tongued dogs razored the sky with their howls.

I watched you sleeping and wondered—could you hear them, too, rising from alleyways and churchyards and abandoned warehouses, signaling the arrival of something nameless and foreboding?

You opened your eyes. You fixed your gaze upon me. "Do you remember why I call you Mr. Isn't?" you whispered, running a finger along my collarbone.

I shivered. Outside my window, the blue howling swelled. I could sense the elders drawing near—if I closed my eyes, I could hear them, chanting their liturgies, casting nets made of words that pretended to be light.

"No," I said. "You'll have to remind me. I can't remember anything."

Plein Air (Last Poem)

"Cease your stridulation, good sir," said the conductor. "It's time to disembark."

"You mean 'disambiguate,'" I said.

He smiled and pointed to the door—then the field opened before us: lush grasses, bright ribbon of river in the distance, and a few trees too impressionistic to name—

It was Cezanne who said of Claude Monet that he was "only an eye, but my God, what an eye!"

Why then, in my dream, does a furrier appear with warm blood on his breath? He offers to carry my easel, even prepare my palette, but I know if I let him, I'll have to use earth tones—all those siennas and ochres and umbers. No!

See how the river reflects the sky? I must hold that in my mind, hold it and keep it, though my heart weighs thirty stone.

Was it Plotinus who said, "Life is the flight of the alone to the alone"?

Someone phone my publicist and tell him to get to work!

Consciousness is the tail in the mouth of matter—that's my belief, and it's as good as any.

Mix the colors on the canvas, not on the palette.

Remember, most behavior is inherited, and there is always a name beneath the name you utter.

So take my hand, and walk with me to the river. It isn't far.

Keep telling yourself, "I can almost hear it from here," until you actually believe it, and don't let go until I'm gone.

Big Doin's With All the Fixin's

It was something about time machines and theories of Shakespearean authorship—then the silent auction began.

I groped in the dark for my National Humanities Medal.
Why didn't the doctors catch your beatitude in time?

A telemarketer sneezed.
Adverbs scattered, recklessly.

Amidst a flurry of wind chimes, management launched another sortie against the cognoscenti, huddled in their pensive citadels.

In like manner, the symposium ground to a festive halt,
its pathways of cerebration enshrined for the nonce.

A cloud of tingling numbness descended.

We summoned our bourgeois affections as best we could.
"In America, we die with our boots on," said the jacuzzi salesman.

A voice emerged from the opulent display window:
"The goal, as always, is to increase our discursive potential."

Wait! Who said that? Stand forth and be counted!
But there was only quiet peeping, such as narrators make in their sleep.

Nevertheless, encouraged by edelweiss sightings and emboldened with spiritual sangfroid, we sipped our Mulligatawny soup and waited for the carpet cleaners to arrive.

All seemed well, until something triggered the motion sensors, prompting us to hide a little longer.

Poem in Need of End Notes

I pour my life into cracked vessels, believing I am glue.

This leaves me with vessels full of glue.

The cracks remain visible, but maybe that's the point—an idée fixe, if you will.

Recently, I've observed a proliferation of koi ponds throughout "the neighborhood." Shall I circle each one, wringing my hands like a real poet, reciting in cadenced breaths the Latin names of nearby flora?

Shall I suffer a sea change? Shall I paint a "warm, human" portrait of Aunt Flossie or distribute eiderdown to the Children of Saint Clotilde?

Does anyone know if the corn maze is open for business?

The driverless ice cream truck awash in St. Elmo's fire draws nearer in my dreams. The name of its jingling tune remains just out of reach, and so joins an infinity of angels dancing on the tip of my tongue.

Already, the moon's at half-mast. There's not much on TV: Death dances with my unrequited lovers on every channel.

What this text needs is a good fire sermon—or at the very least, some commercial-free gravitas, delivered in earnest tones and proffered with good intentions, like a communion wafer!

It's like the graveyard poets used to say: "Too much theory leads to moral relativism, which leads to totalitarianism, which is bound to hurt somebody's feelings."

Of course, the same is true for too little theory.

Excuse me—did I say "true"? What I meant to say is "Anyone lived in a pretty why town."

Now would somebody please pass the preserves? I'd like to spread something sweet on this toast before the Thracian women finish softball practice and darken everybody's door, shrieking their victory songs and demanding we buy scratch-off tickets.

I already have a drawer full, and I haven't won anything yet.

Ontological Overbite

They tell me that God is a ventriloquist's dummy in the lap of a mime—but what does that prove?

Somewhere, I'm reminded, a forlorn little man sits in the dark, stirring a goblet of nacre, crying shuttlecock tears, and muttering the word "splenetic" over and over till his voice goes hoarse.

Fortunately, thanks to this ceremony involving castanets and Propofol, I can claim with reasonable certainty that he's no longer me.

The Diagnosis

1.

If night is for lovers, then why must it administer starlight through a syringe?

Why must the moon press a cold stethoscope to my chest?

And you, with your four dipsticks, one for each humour—you've been dog-earing pages in The Book of Symptoms since the night you called me "Stammering Pete."

You say I've got the wrong-color accordion; my umbrellas won't sing. My spleen doesn't float like it should.

I've got a cross-eyed heart and too much Leviticus in my brain.

My uvula's aslant; I have a saltshaker for a tongue.

Someone's been reading dime store novels to my pituitary, and now I'm weepy and semi-mystical and wish nightingales were indigenous.

"But what does it all mean?" I ask you. "What do these symptoms portend?"

"Stammering Pete," you say, "we have to run more tests."

2.

"Diagnosis": from the Greek dia (apart) + gignoskein (recognize, know). The flux of everything, pulled apart by the prism of the senses.

And then, each part affixed to a word or words—a pin for every butterfly.

The body as text. Pain as misreading.

The prism of language, overlaying that of the senses—and sometimes substituting for them, as now.

"The Greeks had words for eight types of love," you say, "but no single word for 'love' in general. Kind of like the Eskimos with 'snow.'"

"Which word would you choose?" I ask. And then, "Say, what's that needle for?"

"If you multiply the eight types of love times the four humours, you have thirty-two possibilities," you say. "Once this is understood, we'll know where to apply the leeches more effectively."

I look at you standing there in your gold lamay lab jacket.

What's the Greek word for "minnows breaking the surface of a lake beneath my skin"?

What's the word for "xylophone spine"? For "There's a Theremin in my groin"?

Why do I feel like a dozen characters out of Ovid all at once?

Why have the gods turned into glass, and why am I bleeding flowers?

"The problem could lie with your root metaphors," you say, "—you know, the ones you live by. They may not be shared by the culture at large. That would explain your disease, not to mention your choice of wardrobe and your ambivalence toward any sort of narrative."

"But I don't understand. I merely seek the convulsive beauty beneath the façade of appearances," I say.

"Mm-hmm. Well, as long as you're strapped to this gurney, we may as well conduct a biopsy or two," you reply. "If for nothing else, then for old time's sake. And by the way, I'll be using a local anesthetic because it's vital that you maintain consciousness throughout the procedure. Understand?"

"I think so."

"Good. It might help to close your eyes."

But they're already closed.

I feel the cold wetness of what I assume is some kind of antiseptic. "Okay. You're going to feel a little pinch," you tell me.

I do.

3.

Someone is reading aloud from *The Book of Symptoms*.

"Do you believe night is for lovers, that the wings of desire—gold-veined and diaphanous—can survive machine-washing, or that these death's head moth cocoons your significant other's been leaving under your pillow represent 'turning points' in your 'relationship'?

"Do you sometimes confuse 'mode' and 'genre'?

"Do you believe le mot juste is, more often than not, a gerund?

Do you believe the heart is a spiraling stair, that it has its own elevator music, and that its outlook is primarily medieval?

"Do your mirrors catch fire?

"Do you often find yourself narrating something that isn't quite a story?

"Does your imaginary lover call you 'Stammering Pete'?

"Do you experience synesthesia whenever the moon goes behind a cloud?

"Do you believe that in some poems the butterfly's wing tears loose from its pin and beats frantically against the page?

"Do you believe the final word is ash, and we never hear it spoken, though it's written everywhere?"

"Yes," I say. "Yes to everything."

"And do you believe your eyes are still closed—or are you just pretending?"

"Ah," I say. "Doc, I think you're on to something."

The Interrogation

The interrogation continues. Have I told them everything?

Where did I hide the last piece of sponge cake?

Was I responsible for the heteroglossia?

Who transcoded the leader's injunction?

Why is the moonlight "callow"?

"These aren't the right questions," I said. "And what's more, I'm not the one you should be asking."

"Who else would we ask?" they said, and went on.

Why the obsession with shoehorns and bladderwort?

What did I mean by "the umlauts of your love-making"?

Are the spores political?

How can a notion of "self" be based on origami?

When did I last speak to the carousel operator, and what secrets did he share? Or was it "she"?

Was I to blame for their lack of understanding?

Why did I refuse an interpreter?

When did the mirror stop crying—and what song is it singing now? Or is it something other than a song? How could they be certain what I meant by "song"? By "mirror"? By "stop"?

What did I do with the gravedigger's doll after the bris?

Did I find your high school picture vertiginous?

How often did money change hands?

Who initiated the communication?

When the tide comes in, how high will the water go? Will it "cover everything," like my dead father said in a dream? What did he mean by that? Why was he smiling when he said it?

The Ordinary

The moment for which there is no name passed.

I had erased all I wanted to, maybe more than I needed to.

The sunlight slanting through the trees made no promises, while around the feeder small gray birds huddled like Dickens orphans. The blue sky stretched tight as a drum above me—no clouds for Baudelaire.

I could feel the medicine taking effect. My heartbeat slowed. The ordinary descended: ordinary dew on ordinary grass, ordinary gutters, ordinary houses on ordinary streets. Ordinary dogs barking. Ordinary children shouting.

Everything seemed so easily named. How could anyone bear it?

"The ordinary is allegorical, too," said the angel crouched in the briars.

The gray birds lifted as one and began to circle his head. "Shh," they said. "Shh."

Acknowledgements:

"Frigidaire," "Summer on Neptune," and "About My Last Poem..." first appeared in *Doubly Mad*.

"The Interrogation" first appeared in *Stone Canoe*.

"The Allegorist," "How Is Your Tuesday?", and "Yes-Man" first appeared in *SurVision*.

"Frank's Bad Day" and "The Problem With Me No. 152" are slated to appear in *Glimpse* in early 2023.

About the Poet:

Thomas Townsley has published three collections of poetry, *Reading the Empty Page*, *Night Class for Insomniacs*, and *Holding a Seance by Myself*, as well as a chapbook, *Tangent of Ardency*. Educated at Syracuse University, he has had a diverse career which includes work as a blues harmonica musician, radio show host, and professor. Currently, he teaches English, Philosophy, and Creative Writing at Mohawk Valley Community College. His poetry has appeared in several journals, most recently in *SurVision* and *Doubly Mad*.

I Pray This Letter Reaches You In Time is printed using the Avenir font family. Avenir was designed by Adrian Frutiger in 1987. Book design by William Welch. Printed by Lulu.

www.ingramcontent.com/pod-product-compliance
Lightning Source LLC
Chambersburg PA
CBHW031638160426
43196CB00006B/465